Poor Richard's Almanack

Poor Richard's

𝕬lmanack

BEING the choicest *Morsels* of WIT and WISDOM, written during the Years of the Almanack's publication, By that well-known *Savant*, DR. BENJAMIN FRANKLIN of Philadelphia.

Published in MOUNT VERNON, *at the Sign of* THE PETER PAUPER PRESS, with numerous quaint CUTS by an Unknown Hand

COURTEOUS READER:

It is hardly Necessary to state, that Franklin did not originate all the Sayings of Poor Richard. He himself tells us, that they were the "Wisdom of many Ages and Nations." Any One, familiar with Bacon, Rochefoucauld, and Rabelais, as well as Others, will recognize old Friends in Some of these Sayings, while a Study of the Collections of Proverbs, made in the early part of the eighteenth Century, by Ray and Palmer, will reveal the probable Source from which Poor Richard pilfer'd. Yet, with but few Exceptions, these Maxims and Aphorisms had been filter'd through Franklin's Brain, and were ting'd with that Mother Wit, which so strongly and individually marks so Much that he said and wrote.

PAUL LEICESTER FORD

Poor Richard's

❧ Almanack ❧

Wⁱᵗʰ the old Almanack and the old Year,
Leave thy old Vices, tho' ever so dear.

Many a long dispute among Divines may be thus abridged, It is so: It is not so; It is so: It is not so.

Ill Customs & bad Advice are seldom forgotten.

Men meet, Mountains never.

One good Husband is worth two good Wives; for the scarcer things are, the more they're valued.

He that riseth late, must trot all day, and shall scarce overtake his business at night.

He that speaks ill of the Mare, will buy her.

Fish and Visitors stink after three days.

How few there are who have courage enough to own their Faults, or resolution enough to mend them!

A country man between two lawyers, is like a fish between two cats.

The miser's cheese is wholesomest.

Love and Lordship hate companions.

There's many men forget their proper station
And still are meddling with the administration
Of government; that's wrong and this is right,
And such a law is out of reason quite;
Thus, spending too much thought on state affairs,
The business is neglected, which is theirs.
So some fond traveller gazing at the stars,
Slips in next ditch, and get a dirty arse.

He that can compose himself, is wiser than he that composes books.

Poor Dick eats like a well man, and drinks like a sick.

After crosses and losses, men grow humbler and wiser.

The worst wheel of the cart makes the most noise.

Well done is better than well said.

Fine linnen, girls and gold so bright,
Chuse not to take by candle light.

There are three faithful friends — an old wife, an old dog, and ready money.

He that can travel well afoot, keeps a good horse.

Who has deceiv'd thee so oft as thy self?

William, because his wife was something ill,
Uncertain in her health, indifferent still,
He turn'd her out of doors without reply:
I ask'd if he that act could justify.
In sickness and in health, says he, I am bound
To keep her; when she's worse or better found,
I'll take her in again; and now you'll see,
She'll quickly either mend or end, says he.

A traveller should have a hog's nose, a deer's legs, and an ass's back.

No better relation than a prudent and faithful friend.

There are no ugly loves, nor handsome prisons.

At the working man's house hunger looks in, but dares not enter.

A good lawyer, a bad neighbour.

Certainly these things agree, the priest, the lawyer
    and death, all three;
Death takes both the weak and the strong,
The lawyer takes from both right and wrong,
And the priest from the living and dead has his fee.

He that would have a short Lent, let him borrow money to be repaid at Easter.

Eat few Suppers, and you'll need few Medicines.

If Passion drives, let Reason hold the Reins.

You will be careful, if you are wise, how you touch men's Religion, or Credit, or Eyes.

After Fish, Milk do not wish.

To err is human, to repent divine; to persist devilish.

Bright as the day and as the morning fair,
Such Cloe is, and common as the air.

Here comes Glib-Tongue: who can out-flatter a Dedication; and lie, like ten Epitaphs.

Money & Man a mutual Friendship show:
Man makes false Money, Money makes Man so.

Industry pays Debts, Despair encreases them.

Hope and a Red-Bag, are Baits for Men and Mackerel.

Speak with contempt of none, from slave to king,
The meanest Bee hath, and will use, a sting.

They who have nothing to trouble them, will be troubled at nothing.

Beware, beware; he'll cheat without scruple, who can without fear.

WISE MEN LEARN BY OTHERS' HARMS; FOOLS BY THEIR OWN

Declaiming against Pride, is not always a Sign of Humility.

Neglect kills Injuries, Revenge increases them.

Nine men in ten are suicides.

Keep Conscience clear, Then never fear.

Doing an Injury puts you below your Enemy; Revenging one makes you but even with him; Forgiving it sets you above him.

Great Good-nature, without Prudence, is a great Misfortune.

Do me the favour to deny me at once.

There is much money given to be laught at, though the purchasers don't know it; witness A's fine horse, and B's fine house.

He that would live in peace and at ease, must not speak all he knows, nor judge all he sees.

The use of money is all the advantage there is in having money.

For 6£ a year you may have use of 100£, if you are a man of known prudence and honesty.

He that spends a groat a-day idly, spends idly above 6£ a year, which is the price of using 100£.

He that wastes idly a groat's worth of his time per day one day with another, wastes the privilege of using 100£ each day.

He that idly loses 5s. worth of time, loses 5s., and might as prudently throw 5s. into the river. He that loses 5s. not only loses that sum, but all the other advantages that might be made by turning it in dealing, which, by the time a young man becomes old, amounts to a comfortable bag of money.

A penny saved is two pence clear. A pin a-day is a groat a-year. Save and have.

Every little makes a mickle.

Keep thy shop, and thy shop will keep thee.

He that goes far to marry, will either deceive or be deceived.

If you would have guests merry with cheer, be so yourself, or so at least appear.

The poor man must walk to get meat for his stomach, the rich man to get a stomach for his meat.

Avarice and happiness never saw each other, how then should they become acquainted.

The family of fools is ancient.

The king's cheese is half wasted in parings; but no matter, 'tis made of the people's milk.

There's many witty men whose brains can't fill their bellies.

Be slow in chusing a friend, slower in changing.

A ship under sail and a big-bellied woman, are the handsomest two things that can be seen common.

When ♂ and ♀ in conjunction lie,
Then, maids, whate'er is ask'd of you, deny.

Necessity never made a good bargain.

Let all Men know thee, but no man know thee thoroughly: Men freely ford that see the shallows.

Ah simple Man! when a boy two precious jewels were given thee, Time and good Advice; one thou hast lost, and the other thrown away.

If you'd be wealthy, think of saving, more than of getting: The Indies have not made Spain rich, because her Outgoes equal her Incomes.

When Knaves fall out, honest men get their goods: When Priests dispute, we come at the Truth.

Experience keeps a dear school, yet Fools will learn in no other.

To-morrow you'll reform, you always cry;
In what far country does this morrow lie,
That 'tis so mighty long ere it arrive?
Beyond the *Indies* does this morrow live?
'Tis so far-fetched, this morrow, that I fear
'Twill be both very old and very dear.

How many observe Christ's Birth-day; How few his Precepts! O! 'tis easier to keep Holidays than Commandments.

He that drinks his Cyder alone, let him catch his Horse alone.

Who is rich? He that rejoices in his Portion.

The Devil wipes his Breech with poor Folks' Pride.

Monkeys, warm with envious spite, their most obliging friends will bite.

A lawyer being sick, and extream ill,
Was moved by his friends to make his will,
Which soon he did, gave all the wealth he had,
To frantic persons, lunatick and mad.
And to his friends this reason did reveal,
(That they might see with equity he'd deal,)
From madmen's hands I did my wealth receive,
Therefore that wealth to madmen's hands I leave.

Half Wits talk much but say little.

A . . . they say has wit; for what? For writing?
——No,—for writing not.

An open foe may prove a curse; but a pretended friend is worse.

On his death bed poor Lubin lies;
   His spouse is in despair;
With frequent sobs, and mutual cries
   They both express their care.
A diff'rent cause, says parson *Sly*,
   The same effect may give,
Poor *Lubin* fears that he shall die;
   His wife — that he may live.

A little well-gotten will do us more good, than lordships and scepters by Rapine and Blood.

Wealth is not his that has it, but his that enjoys it.

'Tis easy to see, hard to foresee.

In a discreet man's mouth a publick thing is private.

Let thy maid-servant be faithful, strong, and homely.

Here comes Courage! that seized the lion absent, and ran away from the present mouse.

Cæsar did not merit the triumphal car more than he that conquers himself.

Altho' thy teacher act not as he preaches,
Yet ne'ertheless, if good, do what he teaches;
Good counsel, failing men may give, for why,
He that's aground knows where the shoal doth lie.

Nor eye in a letter, nor hand in a purse, nor ear in the secret of another.

He that buys by the penny, maintains not only himself, but other people.

My old friend Berryman often, when alive,
Taught others thrift, himself could never thrive:
Thus like the whetstone, many men are wont
To sharpen others while themselves are blunt.

Great talkers should be cropp'd, for they have no need of ears.

Those who in quarrels interpose, must often wipe a bloody nose.

Where yet was ever found the mother, who'd change her booby for another?

He that hath a Trade, hath an Estate.

There are no fools so troublesome as those that have wit.

Late Children, early Orphans.

Quarrels never could last long, if on one side only lay the wrong.

Up, sluggard, and waste not life; in the grave will be sleeping enough.

Strange! that a Man who has wit enough to write a Satyr, should have folly enough to publish it.

Have you somewhat to do to-morrow, do it today.

The painful Preacher, like a candle bright, Consumes himself in giving others Light.

Speak and speed: the close mouth catches no flies.

Visit your Aunt, but not every Day; and call at your Brother's, but not every night.

Tart Words make no Friends: a spoonful of honey will catch more flies than a Gallon of Vinegar.

Prayers and Provender hinder no Journey.

> You say you'll spend five hundred pound,
>   The world and men to know,
> And take a tour all Europe round,
>   Improving as you go.
> Dear *Sam*, in search of other's sense,
>   Discover not your own;
> But wisely double the expense,
>   That you may pass unknown.

Give me yesterday's Bread, this Day's Flesh, and last Year's Cyder.

Hear Reason, or she'll make you feel her.

What you would seem to be, be really.

Sloth (like Rust) consumes faster than Labour wears: the used Key is always bright.

Make haste slowly.

Light Gains, heavy Purses.

The Way to see by Faith is to shut the Eye of Reason.

As Pride increases, Fortune declines.

Drive thy Business, or it will drive thee.

HE'S GONE, AND FORGOT NOTHING BUT TO SAY FAREWELL
TO HIS CREDITORS

Changing Countries or Beds, cures neither a bad Manager, nor a Fever.

What's proper is becoming: See the Blacksmith with his white Silk Apron!

The Morning Daylight appears plainer when you put out your Candle.

The most exquisite Folly is made of Wisdom spun too fine.

Neither trust, nor contend, nor lay wagers, nor lend; and you'll have peace to your Lives' end.

The Muses love the Morning.

Thirst after desert—not reward.

An empty bag cannot stand upright.

Happy that Nation,—fortunate that age, whose history is not diverting.

What is a Butterfly? — at best he's but a catterpillar drest.—The gaudy Fop's his picture just.

Tricks and treachery are the practice of fools that have not wit enough to be honest.

Who says Jack is not generous? — he is always fond of giving, and cares not for receiving, — what?—why, *advice.*

Fear not death; for the sooner we die, the longer shall we be immortal.

Whimsical *Will* once fancy'd he was ill,
The Doctor call'd, who thus examin'd *Will;*
How is your appetite? O, as to that
I eat quite heartily, you see I'm fat;
How is your sleep anights? 'Tis sound and good;
I eat, drink, sleep, as well as e'er I cou'd.
Will, says the doctor, clapping on his hat,
I'll give you something shall remove all that.

There are lazy minds as well as lazy bodies.

When you speak to a man, look on his eyes; when he speaks to thee, look on his mouth.

Observe all men; thyself most.

Wish not so much to live long, as to live well.

If any man flatters me, I'll flatter him again, though he were my best friend.

If you have time, don't wait for time.

There's none deceived but he that trusts.

None but the well-bred man knows how to confess a fault, or acknowledge himself in an error.

Drive thy business; — let not that drive thee.

Lalus who loves to hear himself discourse,
Keeps talking still as if he frantick were,
And tho' himself might no where hear a worse,
Yet he no other but himself will hear.
Stop not his mouth, if he be troublesome,
But stop his ears, and then the man is dumb.

There is much difference between imitating a good man, and counterfeiting him.

Wink at small faults — remember thou hast great ones.

Eat to please thyself, but dress to please others.

Search others for their virtues, thyself for thy vices.

Each year one vicious habit rooted out, in time might make the worst man good throughout.

Pay what you owe, and what you're worth you'll know.

Hunger is the best Pickle.

Enrag'd was Buckram, when his wife he beat,
That she'd so often, "lousy knave" repeat.
At length he seized and dragg'd her to the well,
I'll cool thy tongue, or I'll thy courage quell.
Ducking, thy case, poor Buckram, little mends;
She had her lesson at her fingers' ends.
Sows'd over head, her arms she raises high;
And cracking nails the want of tongue supply.

A man in a Passion rides a mad Horse.

Little Strokes, Fell great Oaks.

'Tis hard (but glorious) to be poor and honest.

An empty Sack can hardly stand upright; but if it does, 'tis a stout one!

Daphnis, says *Clio*, has a charming Eye;
What Pity 'tis her Shoulder is awry.

Sound, & sound Doctrine, may pass through a Ram's Horn, and a Preacher, without straightening the one, or amending the other.

Clean your Finger, before you point at my Spots.

He that spills the Rum loses that only; He that drinks it, often loses both that and himself.

Who is strong? He that can conquer his bad Habits.

He that has not got a Wife, is not yet a compleat Man.

Dine with little, sup with less: Do better still; sleep supperless.

A Person threatening to go to Law, was dissuaded from it by his Friend, who desired him to *consider*, for the Law was chargeable. I don't care, reply'd the other, I will not consider, I'll go to Law. Right, said his Friend, for if you go to law, I am sure you don't consider.

If you'd lose a troublesome Visitor, lend him money.

ON T. T. WHO DESTROYED HIS LANDLORD'S FINE WOOD

Indulgent nature to each kind bestows
A secret instinct to discern its foes:
The goose, a silly bird, avoids the fox;
Lambs fly from wolves; and sailors steer from rocks;
A rogue the gallows, as his fate, foresees,
And bears the like antipathy to trees.

To-morrow I'll reform, the fool does say;
To-day itself's too late; — the *wise* did yesterday.

Industry, Perseverance, & Frugality, make Fortune yield.

Fear to do ill, and you need fear nought else.

Ye Party Zealots, thus it fares with you,
When Party Rage too warmly you pursue;
Both Sides club Nonsense and impetuous Pride,
And *Folly* joins whom *Sentiments* divide.
You vent your Spleen as Monkeys when they pass,
Scratch at the mimic Monkey in the Glass,
While both are *one;* and henceforth be it known,
Fools of both Sides shall stand as Fools alone.

George came to the crown without striking a
blow; Ah!—quoth the Pretender, would I could
do so.

Seven wealthy towns contend for Homer dead,
Thro' which the living Homer beg'd his bread.

No wonder Tom grows fat: th'unwieldy sinner
Makes his whole life but one continual dinner.

Lying rides upon debt's back.

Boy, bring a bowl of china here,
Fill it with water cool and clear;
Decanter with Jamaica ripe,
And spoon of silver, clean and bright,
Sugar twice-fin'd in pieces cut,
Knife, sieve, and glass in order put,
Bring forth the fragrant fruit, and then
We're happy till the clock strikes ten.

A man of knowledge like a rich soil, feeds
If not a world of corn, a world of weeds.

The poor have little, — beggars none;
The rich too much — enough not one.

None are deceived, but they that confide.

A Wolf eats sheep but now and then;
Ten thousands are devour'd by men.

To all apparent beauties blind, each blemish
strikes an envious mind.

Thou hadst better eat salt with the philosophers
of Greece, than sugar with the courtiers of Italy.

Against Diseases here, the strongest Fence,
Is the defensive Virtue, Abstinence.
If thou dost ill, the joy fades, not the pains;
If well, the pain doth fade, the joy remains.

Marry above thy match, and thou 'lt get a
master.

Seek Virtue, and of that possest, to Providence
resign the rest.

Promises may get thee friends, but non-
performance will turn them into enemies.

Avoid dishonest gain: no price can recom-
pence the pangs of vice.

Enjoy the present hour, be mindful of the past;
And neither fear nor wish the approaches of
the last.

THERE ARE MORE OLD DRUNKARDS THAN OLD DOCTORS

Harry Smatter, has a Mouth for every Matter.

'Tis a well spent penny that saves a groat.

Many Foxes grow grey, but few grow good.

Content makes poor men rich; Discontent makes rich Men poor.

Different Sects like different clocks, may be all near the matter, 'tho they don't quite agree.

If your head is wax, don't walk in the Sun.

Petty & Witty will wound if they hit ye.

You may be too cunning for One, but not for All.

Genius without Education is like Silver in the Mine.

Poor Plain dealing! dead without Issue.

When painful Colin in his grave was laid,
His mournful wife this lamentation made:
I've lost, alas! (poor wretch, what must I do?)
The best of friends and best of husbands too.
Thus of all joy and happiness bereft:
And with the charge of ten good children left;
A greater grief no woman sure can know.
Who (with ten children) — *who* will have me now?

Many would live by their Wits, but break for want of stock.

You can bear your own Faults, and why not a Fault in your Wife.

Tho' Modesty is a Virtue, Bashfulness is a Vice.

Hide not your Talents, they for Use were made:
What's a Sun-Dial in the Shade?

What signifies knowing the Names, if you know not the Natures of Things?

Tim was so learned, that he could name a Horse in nine Languages. So ignorant, that he bought a Cow to ride on.

Learn of the skilful: He that teaches himself, hath a fool for his master.

Death takes no bribes.

E'er you remark another's sin, bid your own conscience look within.

Anger and folly walk cheek by jole; repentance treads on both their heels.

Well done, is twice done.

Clearly spoken, Mr. Fogg! You explain English by Greek.

Impudent *Jack*, who now lives by his shifts,
Borrowing of driblets, boldly begging gifts,
For twenty shillings lent him t'other day,
(By one who ne'er expected he would pay,)
On his friend's paper fain a note wou'd write;
His friend, as needless, did refuse it quite;
Paper was scarce, and 'twas too hard, it's true,
To part with cash, and lose his paper too.

If evils come not, then our fears are vain;
And if they do, fear but augments the pain.

Pride is as loud a Beggar as Want, and a great deal more saucy.

There are three Things extreamly hard, Steel, a Diamond and to know one's self.

Be not niggardly of what costs thee nothing, as courtesy, counsel, and countenance.

Things that are bitterer than gall,
Physicians say are always physical:
Now women's tongues if into powder beaten,
May in a potion or a pill be eaten,
And as there's nought more bitter, I do muse,
That women's tongues in physick they ne'er use.
Myself and others who lead restless lives,
Would spare that bitter member of our wives.

Man's tongue is soft, and bone doth lack;
Yet a stroke therewith may break a man's back.

Proclaim not all thou knowest, all thou owest, all thou hast, nor all thou can'st.

Sin is not hurtful because it is forbidden, but it is forbidden because it is hurtful.

Nor is a duty beneficial because it is command-ed, but it is commanded because it is beneficial.

O Lazy bones! Dost thou think God would have given thee arms and legs, if he had not design'd thou should'st use them?

Great beauty, great strength, and great riches are really and truly of no great use; a right heart exceeds all.

To bear other people's afflictions, every one has courage and enough to spare.

Epitaph on a Scolding Wife by her Husband:
Here my poor Bridget's Corps doth lie, she is at rest, — and so am I.

A light purse is a heavy curse.

Help, Hands; For I have no Lands.

Dick's wife was sick, and pos'd the doctors' skill,
Who differ'd how to cure th' inveterate ill.
Purging the one prescribed. No, quoth another,
That will do neither good nor harm, my brother,
Bleeding's the only way; 'twas quick reply'd,
That's certain death; but e'en let Dick decide.
"I'se no great skill," quo' Richard, *"by the Rood,
But I think bleeding's like to do most good."*

He's a Fool that cannot conceal his Wisdom.

Great spenders are bad lenders.

All blood is alike ancient.

A true Friend is the best Possession.

No gains without pains.

Fools make feasts and wise men eat them.

A Man without ceremony has need of great merit in its place.

Graft good fruit all, or graft not at all.

Many complain of their Memory, few of their Judgment.

A full Belly is the Mother of all Evil.

The same man cannot be both Friend and Flatterer.

He who multiplies Riches multiplies Cares.

An old man in a House is a good Sign.

Women are books, and men the readers be,
Who sometimes in those book erratas see;
Yet oft the reader's raptured with each line,
Fair print and paper, fraught with sense divine;
Tho' some, neglectful, seldom care to read,
And faithful wives no more than bibles heed.
Are women books? says Hodge, then would mine were
An Almanack, to change her every year.

Those who are fear'd, are hated.

The Things which hurt, instruct.

The Eye of a Master, will do more Work than his Hand.

A soft Tongue may strike hard.

You may talk too much on the best of subjects.

Fear God, and your Enemies will fear you.

Beware of little Expences: a small leak will sink a great ship.

Wars bring scars.

Christianity commands us to pass by injuries; policy, to let them pass by us.

If thou injurest conscience, it will have its revenge on thee.

When man and woman die, as poets sung, his heart's the last part moves, her last, the tongue.

Let thy discontents be thy secrets;—if the world knows them 'twill despise thee and increase them.

Nick's passions grow fat and hearty: his understanding looks consumptive!

Hear no ill of a friend, nor speak any of an enemy.

Pay what you owe, and you'll know what is your own.

Don't overload gratitude; if you do, she'll kick.

Be always ashamed to catch thyself idle.

At 20 years of age the will reigns; at 30 the wit; at 40 the judgment.

If you would keep your secret from an enemy, tell it not to a friend.

They who have nothing to be troubled at, will be troubled at nothing.

Wedlock, as old men note, hath likened been,
Unto a public crowd or common rout;
Where those that are without would fain get in,
And those that are within, would fain get out.

Three may keep a secret, if two of them are dead.

Poverty wants some things, luxury many things, avarice all things.

When Robin now three days had married been,
And all his friends and neighbors gave him joy,
This question of his wife he asked then,
Why till her marriage day she proved so coy?
Indeed, said he, 'twas well thou didst not yield,
For doubtless then my purpose was to leave thee.
O, sir, I once before was so beguil'd,
And was resolved the next should not deceive me.

What's given shines, what's receiv'd is rusty.

A lie stands on one leg, truth on two.

The creditors are a superstitious sect, great observers of set days and times.

Sloth and silence are a fool's virtues.

Great wits jump, says the poet, and hit his head against the post.

Grief often treads upon the heels of pleasure,
Marry'd in haste, we oft repent at leisure;
Some by experience find these words misplaced,
Marry'd at leisure, they repent in haste.

A Brother may not be a Friend, but a Friend will always be a Brother.

Ceremony is not Civility; nor Civility Ceremony.

Among the Divines there has been much Debate,
Concerning the World in its ancient Estate;
Some say 'twas once good, but now is grown bad,
Some say 'tis reform'd of the Faults it once had:
I say 'tis the best World, this that we now live in,
Either to lend, or to spend, or to give in;
But to borrow, to beg, or to get a Man's own,
It is the worst World that ever was known.

Mankind are very odd Creatures: One Half censure what they practise, the other half practise what they censure; the rest always say and do as they ought.

Pride dines upon Vanity, sups on Contempt.

Great Merit is coy, as well as great Pride.

An undutiful Daughter, will prove an unmanageable Wife.

Old Boys have their Playthings as well as young Ones; the Difference is only in the Price.

Hold your Council before Dinner; the full Belly hates Thinking as well as Acting.

Praise to the undeserving, is severe Satyr.

THE TONGUE OFFENDS, AND THE EARS GET THE CUFFING

He is not well bred, that cannot bear Ill-Breeding in others.

Many have been ruined by buying good pennyworths.

Says *George* to *William*, Neighbor, have a care,
Touch not that tree — 'tis sacred to despair;
Two wives I had, but, ah! that joy is past!
Who breath'd upon those fatal boughs their last.
The best in all the row, without dispute,
Says *Will* — Would mine but bear such precious
    fruit!
When next you prune your orchard, save for me
(*I have a spouse*) one cyon of that tree.

When there's no Law, there's no Bread.

Kings and bears often worry their keepers.

Light purse, heavy heart.

He's a fool that makes his doctor his heir.

Ne'er take a wife till thou hast a house (and a fire) to put her in.

He's gone, and forgot nothing but to say fare-well to his creditors.

Love well, whip well.

Great talkers, little doers.

A rich rogue is like a fat hog, who never does good till as dead as a log.

Beware of the young doctor and the old barber.

Eat to live, and not live to eat.

After three days men grow weary of a wench, a guest, and weather rainy.

To lengthen thy life, lessen thy meals.

The proof of gold is fire; the proof of woman, gold; the proof of man, a woman.

After feasts made, the maker scratches his head.

He that lieth down with dogs, shall rise up with fleas.

Take counsel in wine, but resolve afterwards in water.

He that drinks fast, pays slow.

Great famine when wolves eat wolves.

A good wife lost, is God's gift lost.

He is ill clothed that is bare of virtue.

Men and melons are hard to know.

He's the best physician that knows the worthlessness of the most medicines.

Beware of meat twice boil'd, and an old foe reconcil'd.

There is no little enemy.

The heart of the fool is in his mouth, but the mouth of the wise man is in his heart.

Cheese and salt meat should be sparingly eat.

Doors and walls are fools' paper.

Keep your mouth wet, feet dry.

He has lost his boots, but sav'd his spurs.

You cannot pluck roses without fear of thorns, Nor enjoy a fair wife without danger of horns.

God works wonders now and then; behold! a lawyer, an honest man.

We are not so sensible of the greatest Health as of the least Sickness.

A Father's a Treasure; a Brother's a Comfort; a Friend is both.

What maintains one Vice would bring up two children.

A quiet Conscience sleeps in Thunder, but Rest and Guilt live far asunder.

> Deaf, giddy, helpless, left alone,
> To all my friends a burthen grown,
> No more I hear a great church bell,
> Than if it rung out for my knell:
> At thunder now no more I start,
> Than at the whispering of a fart:
> Nay what's incredible, alack!
> I hardly hear my *Bridget's* clack.

He that won't be counsell'd, can't be help'd.

Craft must be at charge for clothes, but Truth can go naked.

Write Injuries in Dust, Benefits in Marble.

What is Serving God?' Tis doing Good to Man.

A Slip of the Foot you may soon recover, but a slip of the Tongue you may never get over.

It is wise not to seek a Secret and Honest not to reveal it.

Cut the Wings of your Hens and Hopes, lest they lead you a weary Dance after them.

In Rivers and bad Governments, the lightest things swim at top.

The Cat in Gloves catches no Mice.

Good Death, said a Woman, for once be so kind
To take me, and leave my dear Husband behind;
But when Death appear'd with a sour Grimace,
The Woman was dash'd at his thin hatchet Face;
So she made him a Court'sy, and modestly sed,
If you come for my Husband, he lies there in Bed.

The Horse thinks one thing, and he that saddles him another.

Love your Neighbour; yet don't pull down your Hedge.

When Prosperity was well mounted, she let go the Bridle, and soon came tumbling out of the Saddle.

In the Affairs of this World Men are saved, not by Faith, but by the Want of it.

Friendship cannot live with Ceremony, nor without Civility.

The learned Fool writes his Nonsense in better Language than the unlearned; but still 'tis Nonsense.

Bite a man, and test his metal.

A fat kitchen, a lean will.

Tongue double, brings trouble.

Many dishes, many diseases.

Would you live with ease, do what you ought, and not what you please.

Better slip with foot than tongue.

People who are wrapped up in themselves make small packages.

Where carcasses are, eagles will gather; where good laws are, much people flock thither.

He that takes a wife takes care.

Lawyers, preachers, and tomtit's eggs, there are more of them hatched than come to perfection.

Neither a fortress nor a maidenhead will hold out long after they begin to parley.

All things are cheap to the saving, dear to the wasteful.

If you ride a horse, sit close and tight, if you ride a man, sit easy and light.

Would you persuade, speak of interest, not of reason.

Happy's the wooing that's not long a doing.

A little house well fill'd, a little field well till'd, and a little wife well will'd, are great riches.

From a cross neighbour, and a sullen wife,
A pointless needle, and a broken knife;
From suretyship, and from an empty purse,
A smoaky chimney, and jolting horse;
From a dull razor, and an aking head;
From a bad conscience, and a buggy bed,
A blow upon the elbow and the knee;
From each of these, good Lord, deliver me.

He that waits upon fortune, is never sure of a dinner.

A learned blockhead is a greater blockhead than an ignorant one.

Marry your son when you will, but your daughter when you can.

Full of courtesie, full of craft.

Eyes and priests bear no jests.

Approve not of him who commends all you say.

Some of our sparks to London town do go,
Fashions to see, and learn the world to know;
Who at return have nought but these to show:
New wig above, and new disease below.
Thus the jack-ass, a traveller once would be,
And roam'd abroad new fashions for to see;
But home returned, fashions he had none,
Only his mane and tail were larger grown.

A Pair of good Ears will drink dry an hundred Tongues.

Danger is Sauce for Prayers.

Serving God is doing good to Man, but praying is thought an easier Service, and therefore more generally chosen.

ON BUYING A BIBLE

'Tis but a Folly to rejoice, or boast,
How small a Price thy well bought Purchase cost.
Until thy Death, thou shalt not fully know
Whether it was a Pennyworth or no;
And, at that time, believe me 'twill appear
Extreamly cheap, or else extreamly dear.

Nothing humbler than Ambition, when it is about to climb.

The discontented Man finds no easy Chair.

Virtue and a Trade, are a Child's best Portion.

Gifts much expected, are paid, not given.

The first Degree of Folly, is to conceit one's self wise; the second to profess it; the third to despise Counsel.

Take heed of the Vinegar of sweet Wine, and the Anger of Good-nature.

The Bell calls others to Church, but itself never minds the Sermon.

IF YOUR HEAD IS WAX, DON'T WALK IN THE SUN

You may delay, but Time will not.

Despair ruins some, Presumption many.

Lost time is never found again.

Nigh neighbour to the squire, poor Sam com-
plain'd
Of frequent wrongs, but no amends he gain'd.
Each day his gates thrown down; his fences broke;
And injur'd still the more, the more he spoke;
At last, resolv'd his potent foe to awe,
A suit against him he began in law;
Nine happy terms thro' all the forms he run,
Obtain'd his cause — had costs — and was *undone*.

Presumption first blinds a Man, then sets him a
running.

Blame-all and Praise-all are two blockheads.

Be temperate in wine, in eating, girls, and cloth, or the gout will seize you and plague you both.

Take this remark from Richard, poor and lame, Whate'er's begun in anger, ends in shame.

What one relishes, nourishes.

Don't think to hunt two hares with one dog.

Fools multiply folly.

All things are easy to industry, all things difficult to sloth.

Beauty and folly are old companions.

He that cannot obey, cannot command.

Where there's marriage without love, there will be love without marriage.

Never spare the parson's wine, nor the baker's pudding.

My love and I for kisses play'd,
She would keep stakes, I was content,
But when I won, she would be paid,
This made me ask her what she meant:
Quoth she, since you are in this wrangling vein
Here take your kisses, give me mine again.

A house without woman and firelight, is like a body without soul or sprite.

Do good to thy friend to keep him, to thy enemy to gain him.

Teach your child to hold his tongue, he'll learn fast enough to speak.

An innocent plowman is more worthy than a vicious prince.

He that is rich need not live sparingly, and he that can live sparingly need not be rich.

Laws like to cobwebs, catch small flies;
Great ones break through before your eyes.

An egg to-day is better than a hen to-morrow.

Drink water, put the money in your pocket, and leave the dry-bellyache in the punch-bowl.

The magistrate should obey the laws, the people should obey the magistrate.

Necessity has no law; I know some attorneys of the same.

Onions can make ev'n heirs and widows weep.

He does not possess wealth, it possesses him.

The thrifty maxim of the wary Dutch, is to save all the money they can touch.

By diligence and patience, the mouse bit in two the cable.

'Tis against some Men's Principle to pay Interest, and seems against others' Interest to pay the Principal.

A great Talker may be no Fool, but he is one that relies on him.

When Reason preaches, if you don't hear her she'll box your Ears.

The Good-will of the Govern'd will be starved, if not fed by the good deeds of the Governors.

A Parrot is for Prating priz'd,
But prattling Women are despis'd;
She who attacks another's Honour
Draws every living Thing upon her.
Think, Madam, when you stretch your Lungs,
That all your Neighbors too have Tongues;
One Slander fifty will beget;
The World with Interest pays the Debt.

Paintings and Fightings are best seen at a distance.

If you would reap Praise you must sow the Seeds, gentle Words and useful Deeds.

Sudden Pow'r is apt to be insolent, Sudden Liberty saucy; that behaves best which has grown gradually.

Many have quarrel'd about Religion, that never practised it.

If man could have Half his Wishes, he would double his Troubles.

ON THE FLORIDA WAR

From *Georgia* t' *Augustine* the General goes:
From *Augustine* to *Georgia* comes our Foes;
Hardy from *Charleston* to *St. Simons* hies,
Again from thence to *Charleston* back he flies.
Forth from *St. Simons* then the *Spaniards* creep;
Say, Children, Is not this your Play, *Bo Peep?*

It is ill Jesting with the Joiner's Tools, worse with the Doctor's.

Children and Princes will quarrel for Trifles.

Success has ruin'd many a Man.

It is not Leisure that is not used.

Haste makes Waste.

From bad Health, bad Conscience, & Parties' dull
   Strife
From an insolent Friend, & a termagant Wife,
From the Kindred of such (on one Side or t' other)
Who most wisely delight in plaguing each other;
From the Wretch who can cant, while he Mischief
   designs,
From old rotten Mills, bank'd Meadows & Mines;
From Curses like these if kind Heav'n defends me,
I'll never complain of the Fortune it sends me.

Philosophy as well as Foppery often changes Fashion.

Ever since follies have pleased, fools have been able to divert.

It is better to take many injuries, than to give one.

Early to bed and early to rise, makes a man healthy, wealthy, and wise.

To be humble to superiors is duty, to equals courtesy, to inferiors nobleness.

Here comes the orator, with his flood of words, and his drop of reason.

If what most men admire they would despise, 'Twould look as if mankind were growing wise.

An old young man will be a young old man.

If you know how to spend less than you get, you have the philosopher's stone.

Sally laughs at everything you say. Why? Because she has fine teeth.

Diligence is the mother of good luck.

Ill thrives that hapless family that shows
A cock that's silent, and a hen that crows:
I know not which lives more unnatural lives,
Obeying husbands, or commanding wives.

Do not do that which you would not have known.

Wish a miser long life, and you wish him no good.

When death puts out our flame, the snuff will tell, if we are wax, or tallow, by the smell.

At a great penny worth, pause a while.

If thou would'st live long, live well; for folly and wickedness shorten life.

Trust thyself, and another shall not betray thee.

Doris a widow past her prime,
Her spouse long dead, her wailing doubles;
Her real griefs increase by time;
What might abate, improves her troubles.
Those pangs her prudent hopes supprest,
Impatient now she cannot smother,
How should the helpless woman rest?
One's gone; — nor can she get another.

He that pays for work before it's done, has but a pennyworth for two pence.

God heals and the doctor takes the fee.

Thou can'st not joke an enemy into a friend, but thou may'st a friend into an enemy.

He that falls in love with himself, will have no rivals.

Grace thou thy house, and let not that grace thee.

He that best understands the World, least likes it.

He that is of Opinion Money will do every Thing may well be suspected of doing every Thing for Money.

Ignorance leads Men into a party, and Shame keeps them from getting out again.

EVERY MAN FOR HIMSELF, ETC.

A Town fear'd a Siege, and held Consultation,
What was the best Method of Fortification:
A grave skilful Mason declar'd his Opinion,
That nothing but Stone could secure the
    Dominion.
A Carpenter said, Tho' that was well spoke
Yet he'd rather advise to defend it with Oak.
A Tanner much wiser than both these together,
Cry'd, *Try what you please, but nothing's like
    Leather.*

Anger is never without a Reason, but seldom with a good One.

An ill Wound, but not an ill Name, may be healed.

A lean Award is better than a fat Judgment.

God, Parents, and Instructors, can never be requited.

Patience in Market, is worth Pounds in a year.

Idleness is the greatest Prodigality.

One Man may be more cunning than another, but not more cunning than every body else.

The Sting of a Reproach is the Truth of it.

Light heel'd mothers make leaden-heel'd daughters.

An Ounce of wit that is bought is worth a pound that is taught.

He that resolves to mend hereafter, resolves not to mend now.

When the well's dry, we know the worth of water.

A good Wife & Health, is a Man's best Wealth.

Virtue & Happiness are Mother & Daughter.

Giles Jolt, as sleeping in his cart he lay,
Some pilfering villains stole his team away;
Giles wakes and cries, — what's here? a dickens, what?
Why, how now? — Am I Giles or am I not?
If he, I've lost six geldings, to my smart;
If not, odds buddikins, I've found a cart.

He that whines for Glass without G, take away L and that's he.

A quarrelsome Man has no good Neighbours.

Buy what thou hast no need of, and e'er long thou shalt sell thy necessaries.

If you want a neat wife, chuse her on a Saturday.

Nothing brings more pain than too much pleasure; nothing more bondage than too much liberty, (or libertinism).

Sam's wife provok'd him once; he broke her
   crown:
The surgeon's bill amounted to five pounds;
This blow (she brags) has cost my husband dear,
He'll ne'er strike more: Sam chanc'd to overhear.
Therefore, before his wife the bill he pays,
And to the surgeon in her hearing says:
Doctor, you charge five pound, here e'en take ten,
My wife may chance to want your help again.

Read much, but not too many books.

You may be more happy than princes, if you will be more virtuous.

If you would not be forgotten, as soon as you are dead and rotten, either write things worth reading, or do things worth the writing.

Sell not virtue to purchase wealth, nor liberty to purchase power.

Keep your eyes wide open before marriage, half shut afterwards.

Mary's mouth costs her nothing, for she never opens it but at others' expence.

Dorothy would with John be married;
Dorothy's wise, I trow:
But John by no means Dorothy will wed;
John's the wiser of the two.

Don't throw stones at your neighbours', if your own windows are glass.

The excellency of hogs is — fatness; of men — virtue.

Why does the blind man's wife paint herself?

He that sells upon trust, loses many friends, and always wants money.

Lovers, travellers, and poets, will give money to be heard.

He that speaks much, is much mistaken.

Creditors have better memories than debtors.

Two or three frolicks abroad in sweet May,
Two or three civil things said by the way,
Two or three languishes, two or three sighs,
Two or three *bless me's* and *let me die's!*
Two or three squeezes, and two or three towzes,
With two or three hundred pound spent at their
  houses,
Can never fail cuckolding two or three spouses.

Forewarn'd, forearm'd.

GOD HEALS AND THE DOCTOR TAKES THE FEE

Many a Man thinks he is buying Pleasure, when he is really selling himself a Slave to it.

Honest Tom! you may trust him with a house full of untold Millstones.

Think, bright *Florella*, when you see,
The constant changes of the year,
That nothing is from ruin free,
The gayest things must disappear.
Think of your beauties in their bloom,
The spring of sprightly youth improve;
For cruel age, alas, will come,
And then 'twill be too late to love.

There is no Man so bad but he secretly respects the Good.

'Tis a Shame that your Family is an Honour to you! You ought to be an Honour to your Family.

Syl. dreamt that bury'd in his fellow clay,
Close by a common beggar's side he lay:
And, as so mean a neighbour shock'd his pride,
Thus, like a corpse of consequence, he cry'd;
Scoundrel, begone; and hence forth touch me not:
More manners learn; and, at a distance, rot.
How, scoundrel, in a haughtier tone cry'd he;
Proud lump of dirt, I scorn thy words and thee:
Here all are equal; now thy case is mine;
This is my rotting place, and that is thine.

Glass, China, and Reputation, are easily crack'd, and never well mended.

Pray don't burn my House to roast your Eggs.

Some Worth it argues, a Friend's Worth to know; Virtue to own the Virtue of a Foe.

Prosperity discovers Vice, Adversity, Virtue.

Many a Man would have been worse, if his Estate had been better.

We may give Advice, but we cannot give Conduct.

Love and Tooth-ache have many Cures, but none infallible, except Possession and Dispossession.

The ancients tell us what is best; but we must learn of the moderns what is fittest.

Fly pleasures, and they'll follow you.

Since thou art not sure of a minute, throw not away an hour.

As we must account for every idle word, so we must for every idle silence.

I have never seen the Philosopher's stone that turns lead into gold, but I have known the pursuit of it turn a man's gold into lead.

Since I cannot govern my own tongue tho' within my own teeth, how can I hope to govern the tongues of others?

Never intreat a servant to dwell with thee.

Whate'er's desired, knowledge, fame, or pelf,
Not one will change his neighbour with himself;
The learn'd are happy nature to explore,
The fool is happy that he knows no more.
The rich are happy in the plenty given;
The poor contents him with the care of heaven.
Thus does some comfort ev'ry state attend,
And pride's bestowed on all, a common friend.

Time is an herb that cures all diseases.

If you do what you should not, you must hear what you would not.

Never praise your cider or your horse.

He that can have patience can have what he will.

Now I have a sheep and a cow, every body bids me good-morrow.

God helps them that help themselves.

Good wives and good plantations are made by good husbands.

Keep flax from fire, youth from gaming.

There's more old drunkards, than old doctors.

Three things are men most likely to be cheated in, a horse, a wig, and a wife.

Poverty, poetry, and new titles of honour, make men ridiculous.

He that lives well is learned enough.

Kind Katherine to her husband kiss'd these words,
"Mine own sweet Will, how dearly I love thee!"
If true (quoth Will) the world no such affords:
And that it's true I durst his warrant be:
For ne'er heard I of woman good or ill,
But always loved best, her own sweet Will.

He that scatters thorns, let him not go barefoot.

Reading makes a full man — meditation a profound man — discourse a clear man.

The Golden Age never was the present Age.

Nice Eaters seldom meet with a good Dinner.

Most People return small Favours, acknowledge middling ones, and repay great ones with Ingratitude.

As honest *Hodge* the Farmer sow'd his Field,
Chear'd with the Hope of future gain 'twould yield,
Two upstart Jacks in Office, proud and vain,
Come riding by, and thus insult the Swain:
You drudge and sweat, and labour here, Old Boy,
But we the Fruit of your hard Toil enjoy.
Belike you may, quoth *Hodge*, and but your Due,
For, Gentlemen, 'tis HEMP I'm sowing now.

Fond Pride of Dress is sure an empty Curse;
Ere Fancy you consult, consult your Purse.

Youth is pert and positive, Age modest and doubting: So Ears of Corn when young and light, stand bold upright, but hang their Heads when weighty, full, and ripe.

What will not *Lux'ry* taste? Earth, Sea, and Air,
Are daily ransack'd for the Bill of Fare.

'Tis easier to suppress the first Desire, than to satisfy all that follow it.

Don't judge of Men's Wealth or Piety, by their Sunday Appearances.

The Wise and Brave dares own that he was wrong.

The Proud hate Pride — in others.

Celia's rich Side-board seldom sees the Light,
Clean is her Kitchen, and her Spits are bright;
Her Knives and Spoons, all rang'd in even Rows,
No Hands molest, nor Fingers discompose:
A curious Jack, hung up to please the Eye,
Forever still, whose Flyers never fly:
Her Plates unsully'd shining on the Shelf;
For *Celia* dresses nothing, but *herself*.

Drunkenness, that worst of Evils, makes some men Fools, some Beasts, some Devils.

For want of a Nail the Shoe is lost; for want of a Shoe the Horse is lost; for want of a Horse the Rider is lost.

The busy man has few idle Visitors; to the boiling Pot the Flies come not.

Calamity and Prosperity are the Touchstones of Integrity.

Kings have long Arms, but misfortune longer; let none think themselves out of her Reach.

'Tis more noble to forgive, and more manly to despise, than to revenge an Injury.

Meanness is the Parent of Insolence.

Love, cough, and a smoke, can't well be hid.

I never saw an oft-transplanted tree,
Nor yet an oft-removed family,
That throve so well as those that settled be.

Let the letter stay for the post, and not the post for the letter.

'Tis better to leave an enemy at one's death, than beg of a friend in one's life.

If you'd have a servant that you like, serve yourself.

Three good meals a day is bad living.

To whom thy secret thou dost tell, to him thy freedom thou dost sell.

He that pursues two hares at once, does not catch one and let's t'other go.

When will the miser's chest be full enough?
When will he cease his bags to cram and stuff?
All day he labours and all night contrives,
Providing as if he'd an hundred lives.
While endless care cuts short the common span;
So have I seen with dropsy swol'n, a man,
Drink and drink more, and still unsatisfied,
Drink till drink drown'd him, yet he thirsty dy'd.

Is there anything men take more pains about than to make themselves unhappy?

The sleeping Fox catches no poultry. Up! up!

Write with the learned, pronounce with the vulgar.

Look before, or you'll find yourself behind.

Tell a miser he's rich, and a woman she's old, you'll get no money of one, nor kindness of t'other.

Sam had the worst wife that a man could have,
Proud, lazy sot, could neither get nor save;
Eternal scold she was, and what is worse,
The devil burn thee, was her common curse.
Forbear, quoth Sam, that fruitless curse, so
   common,
He'll not hurt me, who've married his kinswoman.

Nothing so popular as goodness.

Don't go to the doctor with every distemper, nor to the lawyer with every quarrel, nor to the pot for every thirst.

The rotten apple spoils his companion.

Our smith of late most wonderfully swore,
That whilst he breathed he would drink no more.
But since, I know his meaning, for I think,
He meant he would not breathe whilst he did
   drink.

Marry your daughter and eat fresh fish betimes.

I saw few die of hunger; of eating — 100,000.

Friendship increases by visiting Friends, but by visiting seldom.

If your Riches are yours, why don't you take them with you to t'other World?

Cunning proceeds from Want of Capacity.

What more valuable than Gold? Diamonds. Than Diamonds? Virtue.

What knowing judgment, or what piercing Eye,
Can MAN's mysterious Maze of Falsehood try?
Intriguing MAN, of a suspicious Mind,
MAN only knows the Cunning of his Kind;
With equal Wit can counter-work his Foes,
And Art with Art, and Fraud with Fraud oppose.
Then heed ye FAIR, e'er you their Cunning prove,
And think of Treach'ry, while they talk of Love.

If worldly Goods cannot save me from Death, they ought not to hinder me of eternal Life.

'Tis great Confidence in a Friend to tell him your Faults, greater to tell him his.

Talking against Religion is unchaining a Tyger; the Beast let loose may worry his Deliverer.

Ambition often spends foolishly what Avarice had wickedly collected.

Great Estates may venture more; Little Boats must keep near Shore.

YOU MAY BE TOO CUNNING FOR ONE, BUT NOT FOR ALL

The good or ill hap of a good or ill life, is the good or ill choice of a good or ill wife.

Beneath this silent stone, is laid,
A noisy, antiquated maid,
Who, from her cradle talk'd till death,
And ne'er before was out of breath.
Whither she's gone we cannot tell;
For if she talks not, she's in Hell!
If she's in Heaven, she's there unblest
Because she hates a place of rest.

'Tis easier to prevent bad habits than to break them.

Let thy child's first lesson be obedience, and the second will be what thou wilt.

Let thy discontents be secrets.

Blessed is he that expects nothing, for he shall never be disappointed.

Rather go to bed supperless than run in debt for a breakfast.

An infallible remedy for *toothache*, viz. — Wash the root of an aching tooth, in *Elder vinegar*, and let it dry half an hour in the sun; after which it will never ache more.

Beware of him that is slow to anger: He is angry for something, and will not be pleased for nothing.

A nymph and a swain to *Apollo* once prayed,
The swain had been jilted, the nymph been
   betray'd;
They came for to try if his oracle knew,
E'er a nymph that was chaste, or a swain that was
   true.
Apollo stood mute, and had like to be pos'd:
At length he thus sagely the question disclos'd;
He alone may be true in whom none will confide,
And the nymph may be chaste that has never been
   try'd.

Many a meal is lost for want of meat.

When you taste Honey, remember Gall.

God gives all Things to Industry.

Diligence overcomes Difficulties, Sloth makes them.

Neglect mending a small Fault, and 'twill soon be a great One.

All other Goods by Fortune's Hand are giv'n,
A WIFE is the peculiar gift of Heav'n.
Vain Fortune's Favours, never at a Stay,
Like empty Shadows, pass, and glide away;
One solid Comfort, our eternal Wife,
Abundantly supplies us all our Life:
This Blessing lasts (if those that try say true)
As long as Heart can wish — and longer too.

Bad Gains are true Losses.

A long Life may not be good enough, but a good Life is long enough.

Be at War with your Vices, at Peace with your Neighbours, and let every New-Year find you a better Man.

A Change of Fortune hurts a wise Man no more than a Change of the Moon.

Mine is better than Ours.

Love your Enemies, for they tell you your Faults.

Thus with kind words, squire Edward cheer'd his
    friend;
Dear *Dick!* thou on my friendship may'st depend;
And be assur'd, I'll ne'er see *Dick* in want.
But now in debt, and all his assets scant,
Dick's soon confin'd, — his friend no doubt would
    free him:
His word he kept,—in want he ne'er would see him.

Dost thou love Life? Then do not squander
Time; for that's the Stuff Life is made of.

Good Sense is a Thing all need, few have, and
none think they want.

'Tis a strange Forest that has no rotten Wood in 't
And a strange Kindred that all are good in 't.

Mad Kings and mad Bulls are not to be held by
treaties and packthread.

A true great Man will neither trample on a
Worm nor sneak to an Emperor.

When there's more Malice shown than Matter:
On the Writer falls the Satyr.

More carefully the holy book survey:
Your rule is, you should *watch* as well as *pray*.

A Mob's a Mobster; Heads enough but no
Brains.

Tim and his Handsaw are good in their Place,
Tho' not fit for preaching or shaving a face.

When you're an Anvil, hold you still;
When you're a Hammer, strike your fill.

When Knaves betray each other, one can scarce
be blamed or the other pitied.

Fools need Advice most, but only wise Men
are the better for it.

Girls, mark my Words; and know, for Men of
   Sense,
Your strongest Charms are native Innocence.
Shun all deceiving Arts; the Heart that's gain'd
By Craft alone, can ne'er be long retain'd.
Arts on the Mind, like paint upon the Face,
Fright him, that's worth your Love, from your
   Embrace.
In simple Manners all the Secret lies:
Be kind and virtuous, you'll be blest and wise.

Silence is not always a Sign of Wisdom, but
Babbling is ever a Folly.

Content is the Philosopher's Stone, that turns
all it touches into Gold.

Luke, on his dying Bed, embraced his Wife,
And beg'd one Favour: Swear, my dearest Life,
Swear, if you love me, never more to wed,
Nor take a second Husband to your Bed.
Anne dropt a Tear. You know, my dear, says she,
Your least Desires have still been Laws to me;
But from this Oath, I beg you'd me excuse;
For I'm already promised to *John Hughes*.

Friends are the true Scepters of Princes.

Where Sense is wanting, everything is wanting.

He that hath no Ill-Fortune will be troubled with Good.

A Farmer once made a Complaint to a Judge,
My Bull, if it please you, Sir, owing a Grudge,
Belike to one of your good Worship's Cattle,
Has slain him out-right in a mortal Battle:
I'm sorry at heart because of the Action,
And want to know how must be made Satisfaction.

Why, you must give me your Bull, that's plain;
Says the Judge, or pay me the Price of the Slain.
But I have mistaken the Case, Sir, says *John*,
The dead Bull I talk of, & please you, 's my own:
And yours is that Beast that the Mischief has done.

The Judge soon replies with a serious Face:
Say you so? then this Accident *alters the Case.*

For Age and Want save while you may; No morning Sun lasts a whole Day.

He that would travel much, should eat little.

When the Wine enters, out goes the Truth.

Many Princes sin with David, but few repent with him.

The hasty Bitch brings forth blind Puppies.

Two dry Sticks will burn a green One.

Praise little, dispraise less.

Don't think so much of your own Cunning, as to forget other Men's: A Cunning Man is overmatched by a cunning Man and a Half.

A year of Wonders now behold!
Britons despising *Gallic* Gold!
A Year that stops the *Spanish* Plunders!
A Year that they must be Refunders!
A Year that sets our Troops a marching!
A Year secures our Ships from Searching!
A Year that Charity's extended!
A Year that *Whig* and *Tory*'s blended!
Amazing Year! that we're defended!

You may give a Man an Office, but you cannot give him Discretion.

A Child thinks 20 Shillings and 20 Years can scarce ever be spent.

Willows are weak, but they bind the Faggot.

He that doth what he should not, shall feel what he would not.

To be intimate with a foolish Friend, is like going to Bed to a Razor.

Little Rogues easily become great Ones.

You may sometimes be much in the wrong, in owning your being in the right.

THREE MAY KEEP A SECRET, IF TWO OF THEM ARE DEAD

He is a Governor that governs his Passions, and he a Servant that serves them.

Virtue may not always make a Face handsome, but Vice will certain make it ugly.

Prodigality of Time produces Poverty of Mind as well as of Estate.

The first Mistake in public Business, is the going into it.

He that's content hath enough. He that complains has too much.

Pride gets into the Coach, and Shame mounts behind.

A full Belly make a dull Brain.

The Muses starve in a Cook's Shop.

Spare and have is better than spend and crave.

Good-Will, like the Wind, bloweth where it listeth.

EPITAPH ON A CLERGYMAN

Here lies, who need not here be nam'd,
For Theologic Knowledge fam'd;
Who all the Bible had by rote,
With all the Comments Calvin *wrote;*
Parsons and Jesuits could confute,
Talk Infidels and Quakers mute,
To every Heretick a foe;
Was he an honest man? —— *So, so.*

The Honey is sweet, but the Bee has a Sting.

He makes a foe, who makes a jest.

Employ thy time well, if thou meanest to gain leisure.

A flatterer never seems absurd: The flatter'd always takes his word.

Lend money to an enemy, and thou'lt gain him; to a friend, and thou'lt lose him.

Rob not God, nor the Poor, lest thou ruin thyself; The Eagle snatcht a Coal from the Altar, but it fired her Nest.

Half Hospitality opens his Door and shuts up his Countenance.

Liberality is not giving much, but giving wisely.

Suspicion may be no fault, but showing it may be a great one.

A good Example is the best Sermon.

My sickly spouse, with many a sigh
Once told me, — *Dicky*, I shall die:
I griev'd, but recollected strait,
'Twas bootless to contend with fate:
So resignation to Heaven's will
Prepar'd me for succeeding ill;
'Twas well it did; for on my life,
'Twas Heaven's will to spare my wife.

If Jack's in love, he's no Judge of Jill's Beauty.

Most fools think they are only ignorant.

Pardoning the Bad, is injuring the Good.

Wealth and Content are not always Bedfellows.

Wise Men learn by others' harms; Fools by their own.

The end of Passion is the beginning of Repentance.

Words may shew a man's Wit, but Actions his Meaning.

He that has a Trade has an Office of Profit and Honour.

Be civil to all; sociable to many; familiar with few; Friend to one; Enemy to none.

Vain-glory flowereth, but beareth no Fruit.

The diligent Spinner has a large Shift.

Sylvia while young, with ev'ry Grace adorn'd,
Each blooming Youth, and fondest Lover scorn'd:
In Years at length arriv'd at Fifty-nine,
She feels Love's Passions as her Charms decline:
   Thus Oaks a hundred Winters old
     Just as they now expire,
   Turn Touchwood, doated, grey and old,
     And at each Spark take Fire.

A wise Man will desire no more than what he may get justly, use soberly, distribute chearfully and leave contentedly.

A false Friend and a Shadow attend only while the Sun shines.

To-morrow every Fault is to be amended; but that To-morrow never comes.

Plough deep while Sluggards sleep; and you shall have Corn to sell and to keep.

Laziness travels so slowly that Poverty soon overtakes him.

He that by the Plough would thrive, himself must either hold or drive.

Knaves & Nettles are akin; stroak 'em kindly, yet they'll sting.

Life with Fools consists in Drinking; with the wise Man, living's Thinking.

The generous Mind least regards Money and yet most feels the Want of it.

The second Vice is Lying; the first is running in Debt.

Lord if our days be *few*, why do we spend,
And lavish them to such an evil end?
Or why if they be *evil*, do we wrong
Ourselves and thee, in wishing them so long?
Our days decrease, our evils still renew,
We make them *ill*, thou kindly mak'st them *few*.

For one poor Man there are a hundred indigent.

Vice knows she's ugly, so puts on her Mask.

A Plowman on his Legs is higher than a Gentleman on his Knees.

Wide will wear, but narrow will tear.

Silks and sattins put out the kitchen fire.

Pride breakfasted with Plenty, dined with Poverty, supped with Infamy.

The Royal Crown cures not the Head-ache.

Shame and the Dry-belly-ache were Diseases of the last Age, this seems to be cured of them.

Some ladies are too beauteous to be wed,
For where's the Man that's worthy of their Bed?
If no Disease reduce her Pride before,
Lavinia will be ravisht at three score.
Then she submits to venture in the Dark,
And nothing now, is wanting — but her spark.

Tho' the Mastiff be gentle, yet bite him not by the Lip.

Act uprightly and despise Calumny; Dirt may stick to a Mud Wall, but not to polish'd Marble.

The Borrower is a Slave to the Lender; the Security to both.

Singularity in the right, hath ruined many: happy those who are convinced of the general Opinion.

Proportion your Charity to the strength of your Estate, or God will Proportion your Estate to the Weakness of your Charity.

The Tongue offends, and the Ears get the Cuffing.

Where there is Hunger, Law is not regarded; and where Law is not regarded, there will be Hunger.

The honest Man takes Pains, and then enjoys Pleasures; the knave takes Pleasure, and then suffers Pains.

Biblis does Solitude admire,
    A wond'rous Lover of the Dark;
Each Night puts out her Chamber Fire,
    And only leaves a single Spark;
This, worshipping, she keeps alive —
    Warm'd by her Piety, no doubt:
Then, tir'd with kneeling, just at five,
    She sighs —— and lets that Spark *go out*.

Think of three Things — whence you came, where you are going, and to Whom you must account.

There was never a good Knife made of bad Steel.

The doors of Wisdom are never shut.

In escaping from Fire, a Woman, or an Enemy, the wise man will walk, not run.

The Wolf sheds his Coat once a Year, his Disposition never.

Much Virtue in Herbs, little in Men.

Being ignorant is not so much a Shame, as being unwilling to learn.

He that never eats too much, will never be lazy.

Samson, for all his strong Body, had a weak Head, or he would not have laid it in a Harlot's lap.

"I give and I devise" (old Euclio said,
And sigh'd) "My Lands and Tenements to Ned."
Your money, Sir? "My money, Sir! what, all?
Why — if I must — (then wept) I give it *Paul*."
The Manor, Sir? "The Manor! hold," he cry'd;
"Not that — I cannot part with that" — and dy'd.

When a Friend deals with a Friend, Let the bargain be clear and well penn'd, that they may continue Friends to the End.

To be proud of Knowledge, is to be blind with Light.

Get what you can, and what you get, hold; 'tis the Stone that will turn all your Lead into Gold.

To be proud of Virtue, is to poison yourself with the Antidote.

An honest Man will receive neither Money nor Praise that is not his due.

Tell me my Faults, and mend your own.

He that would rise at Court, must begin by creeping.

All would live long, but none would be old.

Nothing dries sooner than a Tear.

Men take more pains to mask than mend.

'Tis easier to build two Chimneys than maintain one in Fuel.

It is Ill-manners to silence a Fool, and Cruelty to let him go on.

These Blessings, Reader, may Heav'n grant to thee;
A faithful Friend, equal in Love's degree;
Land fruitful, never conscious of the Curse,
A liberal Heart and never-failing Purse;
A smiling Conscience, a contented mind;
A temp'rate knowledge with true Wisdom join'd;
A life as long as fair, and when expir'd,
A kindly Death, unfear'd as undesir'd.

He that would catch Fish, must venture his Bait.

One To-day is worth two To-morrows.

Dally not with other Folks' Women or Money.

Work as if you were to live 100 years, Pray as if you were to die To-morrow.

Idleness is the Dead Sea, that swallows all Virtues: Be active in Business, that Temptation may miss her Aim; the Bird that sits, is easily shot.

Drink does not drown Care, but waters it, and makes it grow faster.

Pride and Gout are seldom cur'd throughout.

Having been poor is no shame, but being ashamed of it, is.

The wise Man draws more Advantage from his Enemies, than the fool from his Friends.

A life of leisure and a life of laziness are two things.

Your homely face, Flippanta, you disguise
With patches, numerous as Argus' eyes:
I own that patching's requisite for you:
For more we're pleas'd, if less your face we view:
Yet I advise, if my advice you'd ask,
Wear but one patch: — but be that patch a mask.

A Cypher and Humility make the other Figures & Virtues of tenfold Value.

If it were not for the Belly, the Back might wear Gold.

Let no pleasure tempt thee, no profit allure thee, no ambition corrupt thee, no example sway thee, no persuasion move thee, to do any thing which thou knowest to be evil; so shalt thou always live jollily; for a good conscience is a continual Christmas. Adieu.

THE END